CLASSIC WARPLANES

NORTH AMERICAN
F-86
SABRE

Lindsay Peacock

GALLERY BOOKS

An Imprint of W. H. Smith Publishers Inc.
112 Madison Avenue
New York City 10016

A SALAMANDER BOOK

©Salamander Books Ltd. 1991
129-137 York Way,
London N7 9LG,
United Kingdom.

ISBN 0-8317-1407-7

This edition published in 1991 by Gallery
Books, an imprint of W.H. Smith
Publishers, Inc., 112 Madison Avenue,
New York, New York 10016.

Gallery Books are available for bulk
purchase for sales promotions and
premium use. For details, write or
telephone the Manager of Special Sales,
W.H. Smith Publishers, Inc., 112
Madison Avenue, New York, New York
10016. (212) 532-660.

CREDITS

Editor: Bob Munro
Designers: Flairplan Ltd., England
Color Artwork: ©Pilot Press, England
Three-view, side-view and cutaway
drawings: ©Pilot Press, England
Filmset by: The Old Mill, England
Color separation by Graham Curtis
Repro, England
Printed in Belgium by Proost International
Book Production, Turnhout

AUTHOR

LINDSAY PEACOCK'S working life has been entirely associated with aviation in one form or another, beginning in 1964 with British European Airways and continuing until after the merger with the British Overseas Airways Corporation which saw the formation of British Airways.

Leaving the latter company in the summer of 1976, he opted to pursue a career as a freelance aviation writer and photographer specializing in military subjects. Since then, he has completed several hundred articles which have appeared in aviation magazines published in the United Kingdom and abroad. He is also the author of a number of books, including the Salamander titles "Strike Aces" and "Aerial Firepower", and has contributed text and photographs to many others.

CONTENTS

"THIS model is a tremendous stroke of fortune for us. It puts us way out in front provided the enemy continues to utilize piston engines." So wrote General der Jagdflieger Adolf Galland in a report to Reichsmarschall Göring on the inherent potential of a new turbojet-powered aircraft being developed by Messerschmitt. Less than a month later, in June 1943, what was to eventually become the world's first turbojet-powered fighter to enter operational service was ordered into series production for the Luftwaffe.

The aircraft concerned was the Messerschmitt Me 262, and its debut was but the latest in a series of firsts for the German aviation industry in the fields of rocket- and turbojet-powered aircraft research and development dating back to June 1938, when a Heinkel HeS 3A turbojet had been test-flown beneath an He 118 mother-ship. Just over a year later, on 20 June 1939, the rocket-powered He 176 research air-

craft flew for the first time; followed by the maiden flight of the world's first turbojet-powered aircraft, the He 178, on 27 August 1939.

Both of these aircraft were single-engined designs, but on 2 April 1941, the world's first twin-turbojet aircraft, the He 280, took to the skies. Just as significant was the fact that this was the

Above: Powered by a single HeS 3b engine, and with Erich Warsitz at the controls, the Heinkel He 178 made the world's first turbojet-powered flight in August 1939.

first aircraft to be designated as a jet fighter. It was soon followed by the prototype Me 262, this aircraft taking to the skies on 18 April 1941. The original design of the Me 262 could be traced back to the mid-1930s, but it was a project plagued by setbacks, one of which concerned development of its turbojet powerplants. Indeed, when the prototype undertook its maiden flight, it was powered by a single piston-engine, for delivery of the BMW 003 turbojets had fallen way behind schedule due to problems with their design and operation.

Eventually, the BMW 003s were rejected in favour of Junkers 109–

Left: Superceding the He 178, the twin-turbojet He 280 was dubbed the world's first jet fighter. A host of engine problems led to its demise in the mid-1940s.

004A turbojets, but the whole saga seemed to typify the problems faced by Messerschmitt and the Luftwaffe in getting the most out of the Me 262. To make matters worse, Hitler's insistence that the aircraft be used primarily as a fighter-bomber rather than as an interceptor hindered the Me 262's potential to make a lasting impact on the air war over Germany during 1944–45. It was a classic case of what might have been.

A CHANCE MISSED

For the Allies, such problems were welcome news, for if it had been used properly, the Me 262 had the potential to decimate the massed ranks of Boeing B–17 Flying Fortresses and Consolidated B–24 Liberator bombers being used to pound targets in the heart of Germany. Such encounters did take place, but piston-engined escort fighters were often able to get

Below: Flying for the first time in late-1942, the Bell XP–59A Airacomet represented the United States' cautious entry into the world of jet-powered flight. In all, 66 examples were built.

the better of their jet-powered adversary thanks to better manoeuvrability and superior combat tactics.

The principle escort fighter used by the United States Army Air Force (USAAF) against the Me 262s was the North American Aviation (NAA) P–51D Mustang; but even as the Mustang battled it out with the Luftwaffe fighters over Gemany, NAA designers were looking to the future. The United States had in fact flown a turbojet-powered aircraft as far back as 1

Above: Though possessed of a truly formidable fighting potential as an interceptor, the Messerschmitt Me 262 was criminally misused as primarily a fighter-bomber.

October 1942, when the Bell XP–59A Airacomet conducted its maiden flight, but the aircraft had proved to be a disappointment, with only modest overall performance capabilities. Nevertheless, several manufacturers, including NAA, realized the potential

project on 18 May 1945, when it merited the award of a USAAF letter contract for a pair of prototypes. Performance criteria included a top speed of at least 600mph (965.4km/h), but the straight-winged XP–86, as it was designated, fell a little way short of this figure, estimates at the time alluding to a maximum speed of 582mph (936.4km/h) at 10,000ft (3,050m).

of a fighter powered by the right turbojet engine, and various projects were beginning to take shape. The honour of supplying the first jet fighter to serve operationally with the USAAF fell to Lockheed, whose P–80A Shooting Star entered limited (non-combat) service as World War II drew to a close. But the design team at NAA were also hard at work.

FUTURE FIGHTER

The development of NAA's new fighter began in the closing stages of World War II, but early design studies bore little more than a passing resemblance to what eventually emerged from the company's factory at Inglewood, California, in the autumn of 1947. Preliminary work predated that event by almost three years and effectively got under way in November 1944 at a time when NAA was actively engaged in a jet fighter development project for the US Navy. Known by the company as the Model NA–134, the Navy machine was destined to enter operational service with elements of

Right: Designed for the US Navy, the portly North American Aviation FJ–1 Fury provided designers with a working basis from which to develop the XP–86.

the Fleet as the FJ–1 Fury, and in view of the almost concurrent development timescale, it was hardly surprising that NAA at first opted to pursue a broadly similar design for the USAAF which it referred to as the NA–140, when the latter service identified a need for a new medium-range day fighter which could also be used as an escort fighter and dive-bomber. This was based upon the use of a straight-wing planform with wing-tip fuel tanks in similar fashion to the Lockheed P–80 Shooting Star's wing configuration.

The model NA–140 made the transition from being merely a promising

In the following month, the NAA design team that was responsible for the XP–86 project took a long hard look at some of the German research data (especially that relating to the fully-swept Me 262 design) which was now beginning to find its way back to the USA. They realized very quickly that the use of a swept-wing planform would theoretically permit the speed requirement to be satisfied and, indeed, exceeded by a quite handsome margin. There were risks, however, especially with regard to stability, German engineers having failed to overcome these problems although

Finalizing the design and construction of the prototypes kept NAA occupied for nearly two years, notable milestones that were passed and events that occurred during this period including service approval of the cockpit mock-up on 28 February 1946; addition of a third prototype to the existing contract on 20 June 1946; release of engineering drawings for the prototypes on 9 August 1946; and, perhaps most importantly of all, approval to move ahead with production of an initial batch of 33 P–86As on 20 December 1946. Many of these

Above: Photographed shortly after its arrival at the Muroc Dry Lake test facility in September 1947, the first XP–86 reveals its sleek and smooth lines prior to its first flight.

and imaginative move that, in years to come, would be stunningly vindicated; but in 1945, despite masses of supportive data, nobody really knew if the gamble would pay off.

Below: Posing for the camera-ship over California's Mojave Desert, the XP–86 reveals its 45deg wing sweepback – as proposed by German engineers for an Me 262 variant.

they were pursuing a number of promising ideas, one of which was the leading-edge slat. If this device could be made to function automatically, then swept wings seemed to be the answer the NAA team were looking for to enhance the XP–86.

Inevitably, there was some resistance, especially at the higher levels of the NAA hierarchy, but authorization was given in August 1945 for wind tunnel testing of this radically new planform. Commencing in September, these tests soon verified the performance gains that could be expected, while the use of a section of bent metal to simulate leading-edge slats indicated that stability and low-speed handling qualities would also be more than satisfactory.

Evidence of this nature paved the way for an entirely new design study and little time was wasted in alerting the USAAF to the much-revised proposal. For its part, the military responded very favourably, and on 1 November 1945 NAA was authorized to proceed with the new, swept-winged version of the XP–86. It was a brave

Above: Not surprisingly, given the as yet unproven qualities of the swept wing, exhaustive tests were carried out, including the use of cotton tufts to study airflow over the wing.

were destined to be employed on test-related tasks, but some did reach front-line operational units and they proved to be the forerunners of close to 10,000 similar production aircraft.

At the time of its roll-out, the XP–86 prototype was revealed to be one of those rare warplanes that look "right" more or less from the outset, its sleek lines as it emerged from the factory for the first time on 8 August 1947 drawing admiring glances from all those who were present. Undoubtedly the most novel feature was the wing, which was swept back at an angle of 45deg (as also were the horizontal and vertical tail surfaces) and which embodied a number of notable innovations, such as double-skin structure and tapered skin so as to save weight while offering good structural integrity. Other features included a pair of hydraulically-actuated air brakes on the aft fuselage sides, which could be employed throughout the entire flight envelope; while the entire rear fuselage section from a point just aft of the wing could be removed to facilitate engine changes. Only four bolts needed to be undone to achieve this and it made it possible for skilled ground crew members to accomplish an engine change in under an hour, although calibration

was still necessary before the aircraft could again venture aloft.

Empty weight of the XP–86 was 9,730lb (15,656kg), which was hardly representative of subsequent production machines for all the prototypes lacked armament. Performance characteristics were also markedly inferior to later aircraft since the three XP–86 prototypes were all powered by either a Chevrolet- or Allison-built J35 turbojet engine. This was significantly less powerful than the General Electric J47 installed in production machines but was nonetheless adequate for the initial phase of flight-test duty.

TESTING TRIALS

Testing of the newest fighter to display American insignia was scheduled to be accomplished at Muroc Dry Lake (now far better known as Edwards AFB), California. Accordingly, the first XP–86 was partially dismantled and moved by road to the test site in the high desert in early September 1947. Once there, it was reassembled and subjected to a complex series of checks before company test pilot George Welch conducted taxi-trials which cleared the way for the XP–86 to take to the skies.

Objectives for the maiden flight were modest, Welch having been instructed to stay aloft for no more

Above: In all, three XP–86s were built, this being the second of the trio. Assigned to a variety of research and test programmes, it was retired from duty in April 1953.

than ten minutes, but the "game plan" fell apart when he attempted to lower the undercarriage for landing. Both of the main gear members operated smoothly enough, but the nosewheel proved to be irritatingly stubborn and refused to lower to its full extent. After 40 minutes of attempting and failing to coax it down, Welch elected to try for a nose-high landing in order to minimize damage. Luck was with him – the jolt as the main wheels made

Below: While other aircraft basked in the Californian sunshine, this F–86A–1 endured −65deg F during tests inside the Climatic Hangar at Eglin AFB, Florida.

contact with the runway was sufficient to free the nosewheel leg, which dropped down and locked in place, allowing the valuable aircraft to roll to an uneventful halt.

The next few weeks were taken up with Category One testing, some 30 flight hours being logged before the USAF took over. Basically entailing a demonstration that the aircraft was able to meet general specification requirements, responsibility for Cat.1 was entrusted in its entirety to Welch, while Cat.2 (initial service assessment) fell to Major Kenneth Chilstrom, a USAF test pilot.

Just over ten flying hours were necessary for Cat.2 trials which were accomplished in early December, the report submitted by Chilstrom being unequivocal in stating the XP-86 to be the best jet fighter tested by the USAF thus far. If the XP-86 was good, and Chilstrom evidently inclined to that belief, then the definitive P-86A (redesignated F-86A when the "P" for Pursuit prefix was replaced by "F" for Fighter on 1 June 1948) looked like being even better.

Further testing of this and the other

Above: Major Robert Johnson (2nd from the right) talks with NAA engineers shortly before setting a world speed record of 670.981mph (1,079.608km/h).

two prototypes kept them busy for the next five years or so, the first prototype earning itself a near-unique niche in the annals of aviation history when, on 26 April 1948, it became the first conventionally-powered aircraft to exceed Mach 1, a speed that had only previously been attained by Charles "Chuck" Yeager in the experimental Bell X-1 rocket-propelled aircraft.

WIN & LOSE

Admittedly Welch had to put the XP-86 into a shallow dive to achieve supersonic speed, but it was still a significant event and it is sad to report that this machine's career was abruptly cur-

tailed when it crashed while on a flight in September 1952.

Within weeks of Welch's supersonic adventure, the first production example of the P-86A had emerged to make a successful maiden flight from Inglewood on 20 May. Powered by a General Electric J47-GE-1 turbojet and known by the company as the model NA-151, this and the second aircraft were the first to be accepted by the USAF (on 28 May 1948) although they were both immediately bailed back to NAA, remaining at Inglewood to perform further development test tasks for some time.

Other production F-86As soon followed, with most of these early specimens being assigned to various experimental establishments. Muroc was a natural "customer" for some; Eglin AFB in Florida had others, including one for climatic trials in the special "cold-weather" hangar; and some others were assigned to the parent company and to the National Advisory Committee on Aeronautics

Below: An impressive display of the F-86A's range of armament (plus fuel tanks), headed by a sextet of .50in (12.7mm) M-3 machine-guns and their rounds of ammunition.

Above: History in the making, as pilots of the 94th FS accept the initial quartet of operational F–86As on behalf of the 1st Fighter Group.

(NACA). Between them, they helped transform what was still largely an unproven but immensely promising warplane into a real weapon for war.

That transformation was accelerated by the first of many massive orders, including one for 188 aircraft on 28 December 1947; but even that seemed insignificant when compared with the order for no fewer than 333 that was placed on the day after the first two production machines were formally accepted by the USAF. Operational

Left: The christening of the USAF's latest fighter led the 94th FS to adopt the title of "*Sabre Dancers*" for its F–86A aerobatic team.

North American F–86 Sabre

Left: Substituting its radar for a nose-mounted receptacle, this Sabre was used in a series of inflight refuelling evaluation flights.

service was, however, still some months away, and it was not until February 1949 that the still-unnamed fighter began to enter the USAF inventory.

Appropriately, the first outfit to re-equip was the 1st Fighter Group (FG), transition beginning with the 94th Fighter Squadron (FS) which had previously operated the Lockheed F–80 Shooting Star. Stationed at March AFB, California, the Group's other two squadrons (27th FS and 71st FS) soon followed suit and a full complement of 80-odd aircraft had been received by the end of May 1949. By then, a "name the fighter" contest had also been held, the winner being selected by 1st FG officers from a "short list" of 78 submissions received in February. Unfortunately, nobody seems to know who was responsible for the winning entry, but regardless of that it stuck and from 4 March 1949 onwards the F–86 was officially known as the "Sabre".

By the end of 1949, two more three-squadron Groups had also begun to acquire Sabres as the trickle of aircraft developed into a flood. At Langley AFB, Virginia, the 4th FG (334th, 335th and 336th FS) was tasked with day air defence of a key sector of the Eastern Seaboard which embraced the huge naval base at Norfolk as well as the nation's seat of government in

Washington DC; while at Kirtland AFB, New Mexico, the 81st FG (91st, 92nd and 93rd FS) was close to Los Alamos, wherein workers in the atomic industry were still striving to perfect nuclear weapons.

Within six months, the USA would again find itself at war, its commitment to the United Nations (UN) cause being tested to the full in the wake of North Korea's invasion of South Korea in June 1950. Within a year, to counter the threat posed by the swept-wing MiG–15 "Fagot", which made its combat debut on the afternoon of 1 November 1950, the Sabre would also be despatched to that distant war zone, and it would not be found wanting.

Right: The Sabre shows its teeth, ripple-firing underwing-mounted 5in (127mm) aerial rockets, up to 16 of which could be carried.

EFFORTS towards enhancing the already impressive capabilities of the Sabre began within months of it entering USAF operational service and led directly to the appearance of the F–86E version, both the F–86B and F–86C (alias F–93) being "blind alleys", while the F–86D "Sabre Dog" emerged as a dedicated all-weather interceptor which is described more fully in Chapter Four.

Fundamentally identical to the initial production variant, work on the F–86E was launched in November 1949, and this model featured one notable innovation in the form of an "all-flying" horizontal tailplane which had a maximum travel of eight degrees up and down measured at the leading edge. Eliminating many of the less desirable side effects of compressibility, the revised tailplane arrangement resulted in more positive control and was warmly welcomed by pilots.

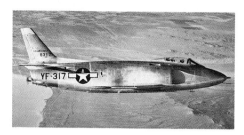

Above: Unofficially known as the F–86C, the YF–93A was intended as a deep-penetration derivative of the F–86A, mating wings from the latter with a new fuselage.

USAF authorization to proceed was swiftly forthcoming, with NAA's initiative being rewarded on 17 January 1950 when the company received a contract for an initial batch of 111 aircraft, the first of which made its maiden flight on 23 September 1950. Evaluation of this new version – and, in particular, the revised control surfa-

Above: The two YF–93As were the only examples of this derivative to fly. Here, the first of the pair sports the original flush configuration air intakes.

ces – kept NAA and USAF test pilots occupied until May 1951, when the F–86E began to enter operational service with Air Defense Command's (ADC) 33rd Fighter Interceptor Wing (FIW) at Otis AFB, Massachusetts.

Within weeks of reaching the 33rd FIW, the F–86E was also despatched to the Korean war zone, where the 4th FIW was still the only Sabre-equipped outfit. Transition to the F–86E was accomplished over a period of several months and it was not until July 1952 that this Wing disposed of its last F–86As; but by then the 51st FIW had acquired combat veteran status with the F–86E, converting to this type from the Lockheed F–80 Shooting Star shortly before the end of 1951.

Combat operations and the generally desperate need for modern fighters prompted the USAF to take the unusual step of ordering 60 aircraft from the Canadair production line in February 1952, these being hastily

Left: Though generally similar to the A-model, the F–86E was the first Sabre to feature an "all-flying tail", which improved control and handling at transonic speeds.

North American F–86 Sabre

FIWs. Further problems encountered in engine production also forced substitution on a later batch of 93 aircraft which emerged from the factory line as F–86E–15s. Handed over between August and December 1952, all 93 were allocated to the Air Training Command (ATC) where they were put to good use helping to speed the output of pilots ready to join the combat-ready USAF forces.

SABRE SURGE

As a consequence of the engine-related difficulties, F–86E production for the USAF was increased threefold, to 336, this figure being boosted by 120 Canadair-built examples. As already mentioned, half of the Canadian aircraft were to see active duty with the USAF, while the other 60 were destined for service with Britain's Royal Air Force (RAF), the aircraft

diverted from Sabre Mk.2 production and delivered to NAA's facility at Fresno, California, where they were fitted with specialized US equipment before being sent to Korea. Known as F–86E–6–CANs, all 60 aircraft were handed over between February and July 1952. In the meantime, US production continued apace to satisfy further contracts, but these were all intended to be for a new model known as the F–86F.

Development of this member of the Sabre family got under way on 31 July 1952, with the major difference relating to the powerplant, for the F–86F was earmarked to take a new version of the General Electric turbojet designated J47–GE–27. Rated at 5,910lb st (2,638kg st), this held out the promise of slightly superior performance and it soon found favour, with a production contract for 109 examples being placed in April 1951 although this was quickly increased to 360 aircraft. Within a few weeks, the decision was also taken to open a second production centre at Columbus, Ohio.

As it turned out, manufacture of the J47–GE–27 engine fell foul of delays and these had a marked impact on the

F–86F programme. Rather than wait, the USAF opted to accept the first 132 aircraft in the F–86F contract with the less powerful 5,200lb st (2,361kg st) J47–GE–13. Duly redesignated as F–86E–10s, these were to be delivered between September 1951 and April 1952, with many of them being sent to Korea for service with the 4th and 51st

PERFORMANCE

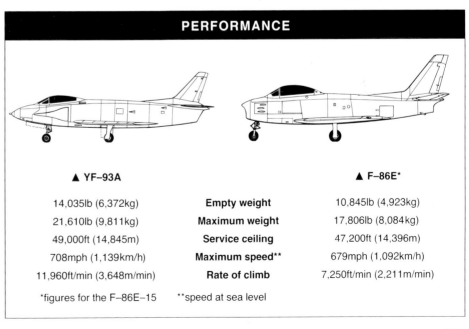

▲ YF–93A		▲ F–86E*
14,035lb (6,372kg)	**Empty weight**	10,845lb (4,923kg)
21,610lb (9,811kg)	**Maximum weight**	17,806lb (8,084kg)
49,000ft (14,845m)	**Service ceiling**	47,200ft (14,396m)
708mph (1,139km/h)	**Maximum speed****	679mph (1,092km/h)
11,960ft/min (3,648m/min)	**Rate of climb**	7,250ft/min (2,211m/min)
*figures for the F–86E–15	**speed at sea level	

Improving the Breed

North American F–86E Sabre Cutaway Key

1 Radome
2 Radar antenna
3 Engine air intake
4 Gun camera
5 Nosewheel leg doors
6 Nose undercarriage leg strut
7 Nosewheel
8 Torque scissor links
9 Steering control valve
10 Nose undercarriage pivot fixing
11 Sight amplifier
12 Radio and electronics equipment bay
13 Electronics bay access panel
14 Battery
15 Gun muzzle blast troughs
16 Oxygen bottles
17 Nosewheel bay door
18 Oxygen servicing point
19 Canopy switches
20 Machine-gun barrel mountings
21 Hydraulic system test connections
22 Radio transmitter
23 Cockpit armoured bulkhead
24 Windscreen panels
25 A–1CM radar gunsight
26 Instrument panel shroud
27 Instrument panel
28 Control column
29 Kick-in boarding step
30 Used cartridge case collector box
31 Ammunition boxes (267 rounds per gun)

32 Ammunition feed chutes
33 .50in (12.7mm) Colt-Browning machine-guns
34 Engine throttle
35 Starboard side console panel
36 North American ejection seat
37 Rear view mirror
38 Sliding cockpit canopy cover
39 Ejection seat headrest
40 Automatic Direction Finding (ADF) sense aerials
41 Pilot's back armour
42 Ejection seat guide rails
43 Canopy handle
44 Cockpit pressure valves
45 Armoured side panels
46 Tailplane trim actuator
47 Fuselage/front spar main frame
48 Forward fuselage fuel tank (total internal fuel capacity 434,4 US gal/1,644 litres)
49 Fuselage lower longeron
50 Intake trunking
51 Rear radio and electronics bay

52 Canopy emergency release handle
53 ADF loop aerial
54 Cockpit pressure relief valve
55 Starboard wing fuel tank

56 Leading-edge slat guide rails
57 Starboard automatic leading-edge slat, open
58 Cable drive to aileron actuator
59 Pitot tube
60 Starboard navigation light
61 Wing tip fairing
62 Starboard aileron

63 Aileron hydraulic control unit
64 Aileron balance
65 Starboard slotted flap, down position
66 Flap guide rail
67 Upward identification light
68 Air conditioning plant
69 Intake fairing starter/generator

70 Fuselage/rear spar main frame
71 Hydraulic system reservoirs
72 Longeron/main frame joint
73 Fuel filter de-icing fluid tank
74 Cooling air outlet
75 Engine equipment access panel
76 Heat exchanger exhaust duct
77 Engine suspension links
78 Fuselage skin plating
79 Engine withdrawal rail
80 Starboard side oil tank (4·75 Imp gal/21,6 l)
81 General Electric J47–GE–13 turbojet
82 Bleed air system primary heat exchanger
83 Ground power connections
84 Fuel filter cap
85 Fuselage break point sloping frame (engine removal)

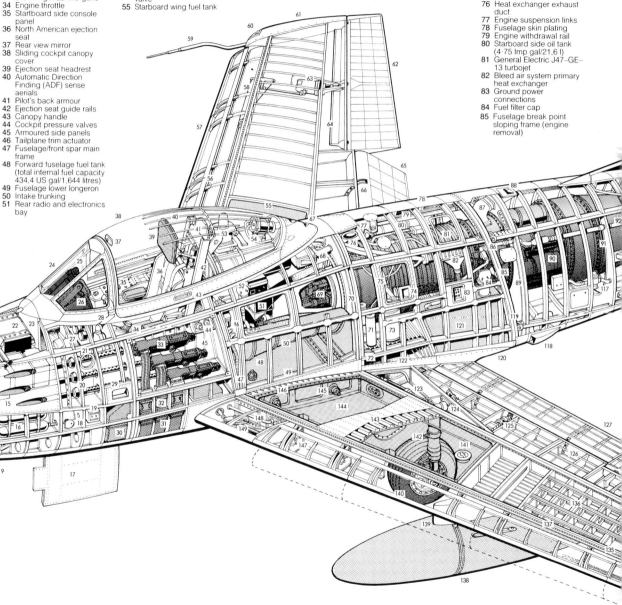

16

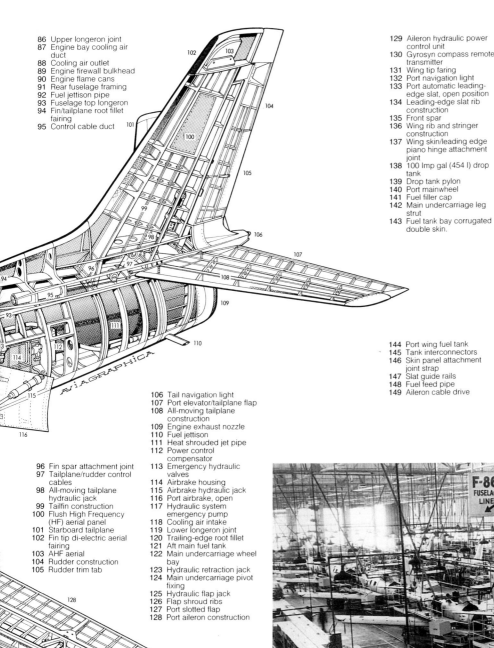

86 Upper longeron joint
87 Engine bay cooling air duct
88 Cooling air outlet
89 Engine firewall bulkhead
90 Engine flame cans
91 Rear fuselage framing
92 Fuel jettison pipe
93 Fuselage top longeron
94 Fin/tailplane root fillet fairing
95 Control cable duct

129 Aileron hydraulic power control unit
130 Gyrosyn compass remote transmitter
131 Wing tip faring
132 Port navigation light
133 Port automatic leading-edge slat, open position
134 Leading-edge slat rib construction
135 Front spar
136 Wing rib and stringer construction
137 Wing skin/leading edge piano hinge attachment joint
138 100 Imp gal (454 l) drop tank
139 Drop tank pylon
140 Port mainwheel
141 Fuel filler cap
142 Main undercarriage leg strut
143 Fuel tank bay corrugated double skin.

144 Port wing fuel tank
145 Tank interconnectors
146 Skin panel attachment joint strap
147 Slat guide rails
148 Fuel feed pipe
149 Aileron cable drive

96 Fin spar attachment joint
97 Tailplane/rudder control cables
98 All-moving tailplane hydraulic jack
99 Tailfin construction
100 Flush High Frequency (HF) aerial panel
101 Starboard tailplane
102 Fin tip di-electric aerial fairing
103 AHF aerial
104 Rudder construction
105 Rudder trim tab

106 Tail navigation light
107 Port elevator/tailplane flap
108 All-moving tailplane construction
109 Engine exhaust nozzle
110 Fuel jettison
111 Heat shrouded jet pipe
112 Power control compensator
113 Emergency hydraulic valves
114 Airbrake housing
115 Airbrake hydraulic jack
116 Port airbrake, open
117 Hydraulic system emergency pump
118 Cooling air intake
119 Lower longeron joint
120 Trailing-edge root fillet
121 Aft main fuel tank
122 Main undercarriage wheel bay
123 Hydraulic retraction jack
124 Main undercarriage pivot fixing
125 Hydraulic flap jack
126 Flap shroud ribs
127 Port slotted flap
128 Port aileron construction

being delivered to the United Kingdom during summer 1953.

Thereafter, production switched to the F–86F, this derivative flying for the first time on 19 March 1952. It was introduced to the inventory in double-quick time, for the USAF accepted an initial batch of six aircraft on 27 March, and by June it was in service with ADC's 84th Fighter Interceptor Squadron (FIS) at Hamilton AFB, California, as well as with the 51st FIW in Korea. Apart from the engine, these initial F–86F–1–NAs were basically identical to the F–86E, but improvements were made throughout the production run which eventually totalled 2,539, including 580 examples specifically associated with the Military Assistance Program. Of the total figure, all bar 300 rolled off the lines at Inglewood, California (1,539 aircraft) and Columbus, Ohio (700 aircraft).

Below: A busy scene on the NAA production line at Inglewood, Ca., with F–86Es taking shape as they gradually make their way around the assembly track.

Improving the Breed

With regard to improvements, the first of these came in June 1952 when the F–86F–5–NA appeared with two beefed-up underwing hardpoints stressed to carry 200 US gal (757 litre) auxiliary fuel tanks in place of the 120 US gal (454 litre) type used thus far. In this configuration combat radius rose significantly, from 330 to 463 miles (531 to 745km), and all subsequent F–86Fs were able to take the bigger fuel tanks. As it turned out, only 16 F–86F–5s were built, and the F–86F–10 was only marginally more numerous with 34 completed. This variant introduced a new gunsight, the more easily maintained and "user-friendly" A–4 unit replacing the A–1CM which had demonstrated an unfortunate tendency to "breed" malfunctions – the last thing that a pilot needed in the heat of battle. Seven F–86F–15s with minor control systems changes followed but quantity production had still to really get into its stride.

At Columbus, the build-up of this "second-source" was slow, following the initial flight of the first F–86F–20–NH in May 1952. By January 1953, however, all 100 on order had been delivered, these introducing a number of new features including armour protection for the mechanized control sys-

SPECIFICATION

North American F-86E Sabre

Dimensions
Length: 37ft 6in (11.44m)
Height: 14ft 9in (4.50m)
Wing span: 37ft 1½in (11.32m)
Gross wing area: 287.9 sq ft (26.75m²)

Weights
Empty: 10,845lb (4,924kg)
Combat: 14,255lb (6,472kg)

Power
1 x Genral Electric J47-GE-13 afterburning turbojet engine

Maximum thrust: 5,200lb st (23.12kN)
Internal fuel: 437 US Gal (1,654 litre)
External fuel: 400 US Gal (1,514 litre)

Performance
Maximum speed, at sea level: 679mph (1,093km/h)
Maximum speed, at 31,000ft (9,455m): 601mph (967km/h)
Service ceiling: 47,200ft (14,396m)
Rate of climb: 7,250ft/min (2,211m/min)
Combat radius: 321 miles (517km)

tem associated with the "all-flying" tail and a revised cockpit arrangement. Up to this point, the Sabre had definitely been viewed as a pure day air superiority fighter, but the next major change was to see it take on the mantle of "fighter-bomber" when it acquired two extra wing stores stations inboard of the existing ones. Able to accommodate the lower-capacity fuel tanks, they alsy had rather more war-like applications in that each could easily carry a 1,000lb (454kg) bomb.

"DUAL-STORE"

Evaluated on the first F–86E–1, this alteration effectively opened the floodgates, with "dual-store" Sabres being ordered in quite massive quantities. Inglewood switched to aircraft with

this potential with effect from the F–86F–30–NA and was rewarded with a contract for no fewer than 967 air-

Above: Although it may appear cluttered by modern standards, the Sabre's cockpit was quite neat for its time. Note the gunsight unit atop the instrument console.

Above: Preparing for another mission with the assistance of his crew chief, a Taiwanese pilot settles into the cockpit of his F–86F. Note the trio of gun muzzle blast troughs ahead.

Left: Clearly making use of the dual-store capability to carry bombs, a pair of South African Air Force F–86Fs head out to attack more Communist targets during the Korean War.

against the Mikoyan Gurevich MiG–15, this was to prove a priceless asset, especially since the MiG fighter had previously been judged superior in a close-in turning fight when flown by pilots of similar ability.

craft, the last 108 actually being completed as F–86F–35–NAs. At Columbus, "dual-store" Sabres made their debut with the F–86F–25–NH (600 built), deliveries from these sources getting under way in October 1952 and January 1953 respectively.

"6–3" SPAN

Even as F–86F production was beginning to accelerate, NAA's project engineers were hard at work examining ways and means to further boost performance of the Sabre, and one of the ideas studied at this time was destined to find acceptance. First proposed by test pilots, a fixed wing leading-edge seemed to do the trick; but NAA took matters a stage further,

electing to utilize a fixed leading-edge in concert with wing dimensions extended by six inches (15.24cm) at the wing root and a further three inches (7.62cm) at the tip.

Commonly known as the "6–3 extension", this alteration inevitably had some impact on airflow characteristics which dictated the provision of five-inch (12.70cm) high wing fences outboard of the underwing hardpoints. In terms of sheer speed, the smoother wing offered only marginal benefit (the maximum speed rose by 9mph [14.5km/h] at sea level, and by a mere 4mph [6.4km/h] at 35,000ft [10,675m]), but this was more than compensated for by improved manoeuvrability, most notably at high altitude and high speed. In combat

WINGS & WEAPONS

Combat gains were to some extent cancelled out by a loss of low-speed characteristics, but it was felt that this penalty was acceptable and the new "hard wing" configuration was incorporated on both production lines with effect from the 171st F–86F–25–NH and the 200th F–86F–30–NA. At the same time, several hundred retrofit kits were purchased in order to pemit all existing F–86Fs to be modified to a common standard.

Below: A classic study of the F–86F at the zenith of its career with the USAF, as 16 Sabres operated by the 531st FBS streak over five of their star-spangled compatriots.

Improving the Breed

Left: Close inspection of the wing leading-edges on these F–86F–35s reveals the incorporation of the five-inch (12.70cm) wing fences fitted to enhance the airflow.

In addition to this new wing configuration, combat experience in Korea emphasized the need for a heavier-calibre weapon possessing much the same rate of fire as the existing battery of M–3 machine-guns, and ten aircraft were modified in Project "*Gun Val*", four F–86F–10s and six F–86F–1s respectively being given four T–160 20mm (0.8in) cannon each as standard armament. As part of the same project, two other F–86F–1s received Oerlikon 20mm (0.8in) guns. In modified form, these were known respectively as the F–86F–2 and F–86F–3, and eight of the former aircraft were used in combat over Korea by the 4th FIW during a four-month evaluation which began in spring 1953.

Although tests and combat evaluation proved promising, the danger of compressor stall meant that only two guns could be fired at the same time, which largely negated the benefit of heavier armament. Nevertheless, several MiGs were known to have been destroyed and the T–160 was ultimately incorporated into the Sabre as the M–39, being fitted to the last 360 F–86Hs built.

The end of the Korean War in the summer of 1953 naturally resulted in reductions in defence spending, but the Sabre still figured prominently on the Pentagon "shopping list", and it was not until the summer of 1954 that procurement of the F–86F for the USAF ended with delivery of the last F–86F–35. Although acquired in only modest quantities, this variant was undoubtedly the most potent F–86F of all, in that it was the only model configured to carry and deliver tactical nuclear weapons. Equipment associated with this mission included the Low Altitude Bombing System (LABS) computer, which was designed to ensure accurate toss- or loft-bombing and to give pilots a reasonable chance of escapting the ensuing blast.

NUCLEAR-CAPABLE

In service, one nuclear store – either the 1,700lb (722kg) Mk.7 or the 1,000lb (454kg) Mk.12, with yields in the 10–60 kiloton range respectively – would be carried beneath the port wing with fuel tanks to starboard. In total, some 264 F–86F–35s were handed over to the USAF, one other aircraft which had been due for delivery in this configuration actually being completed as a TF–86F two-seater.

Development of this trainer version was launched in early February 1953, with authorization to proceed with the modification of a single prototype following on 8 April and the aircraft selected being modified in late-1953. At 42ft 9in (13.04m) it was some 5ft

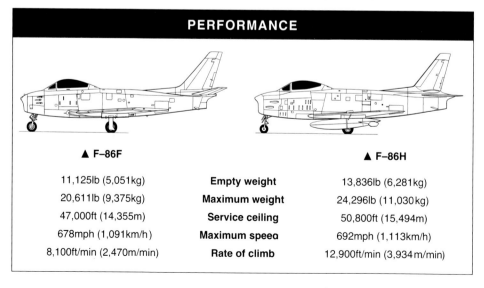

PERFORMANCE

▲ F–86F		▲ F–86H
11,125lb (5,051kg)	Empty weight	13,836lb (6,281kg)
20,611lb (9,375kg)	Maximum weight	24,296lb (11,030kg)
47,000ft (14,355m)	Service ceiling	50,800ft (15,494m)
678mph (1,091km/h)	Maximum speed	692mph (1,113km/h)
8,100ft/min (2,470m/min)	Rate of climb	12,900ft/min (3,934m/min)

Above: The first of two F–86Fs converted as TF–86F dual trainers was unarmed. Sadly, the aircraft was destroyed in a fatal crash on 17 March 1954.

3in (1.60m) longer than the standard Sabre, and it featured a tandem cockpit layout with the student pilot seated in front. Other changes included moving the wing position forward by eight inches (20cm), but apart from a lack of armament and a clamshell canopy it was basically similar to the single-seat F–86F. Aloft for its maiden flight on 14 December 1953, the prototype was to be destroyed during its ninth flight on 17 March 1954.

TRAINER TWO

Within a week, approval was given for construction of a second TF–86F, and this was based on what would have been the last F–86F–35. This time, armament was installed in the shape of two .50in (12.7mm) calibre machine-guns, and it could also carry bombs or drop tanks. Rather longer-lived than its predecessor, this TF–86F flew for the first time on 5 August 1954 and eventually joined the Air Force Flight Test Centre (AFFTC) at Edwards AFB, where it served as a high-speed chase aircraft until the early-1960s.

NAA naturally suggested initiating quantity production of the TF–86F, and Tactical Air Command (TAC) was evidently in favour at one time, but the

USAF rejected the idea on 7 February 1955 when it revealed that it was considering going ahead with procurement of a two-seat version of NAA's F–100 Super Sabre.

Above: The second and last of the TF–86s reveals the longer fuselage of this model, as well as one of the gun ports for the two .50in (12.7mm) machine-guns.

Above: The mid-fuselage chevron adorning this South African Air Force F–86F may look colourful, but its purpose was serious: to help friendly forces discern the Sabre from MiG–15s over Korea.

Above: Awash in colour for a much more peaceful purpose, this F–86F was one of 28 examples supplied to the Argentinian Air Force in 1960, and subsequently used by the "*Cruz de Sur*" aerobatic team.

Improving the Breed

Above: Time marches on, with one of NAA's next generation of jet fighters, the F–100 Super Sabre (foreground), overlooking a pair of Philippine Air Force F–86Fs.

For the F–86F, that should have been the end of the line, but it received a new lease of life within a few months when it was decided to reinstate it in production specifically for friendly Asian nations under the Military Assistance Program. Some 280 aircraft were covered by two contracts, all being completed as F–86F–40s, and they differed in having extended wing tips and leading-edge slats, which resulted in the Sabre's original low-speed handling characteristics being effectively regained.

An interesting side-effect of the decision to reinstate the Sabre in production concerned the USAF aircraft, and this was to result in the wing configuration being changed yet again, this time for the extended wing tip and leading-edge slat arrangement of the F–86F–40. This was retrospectively installed on all surviving F–86Fs in the USAF inventory, many of these aircraft ultimately finding their way overseas when supplied to friendly nations in the late-1950s. Countries which obtained surplus Sabres in this fashion included Argentina, Ethiopia, Norway, Peru, Portugal, Saudi Arabia, South Korea, Spain and Thailand.

One other derivative was also to see

service with the USAF but this was a very different beast entirely, the F–86H being perceived primarily as a fighter-bomber rather than as an air superiority fighter with a secondary air-to-ground capability. Development of the F–86H began on 16 March 1951 with a view to producing an aircraft able to carry a worthwhile payload of conventional or nuclear weapons and offering better overall performance than the F–86F.

H-MODEL MODS

As a direct consequence of that need, a new powerplant was adopted in the form of the General Electric J73 which had a maximum sea level rating of

Above: Emblazoned with its model designation, the F–86H featured a deepened fuselage to house the larger air intake fitted to feed air to its J73–GE–3 powerplant.

Above: An impressive line-up of F–86Es at Chaumont Air Base, in France, underscores the Sabre's presence within United States Air Forces in Europe (USAFE).

8,920lb st (4,050kg st), but which required greater mass airflow if optimum performance was to be achieved. This in turn necessitated a fairly major redesign so as to provide greater intake area, something that was accomplished by increasing the depth of the fuselage by six inches (15.24cm), one definite bonus arising from this being that internal fuel capacity rose from 435 to 562 US gal (1,647 to 2,127 litre), with consequent range benefits.

In addition, the tail surfaces were redesigned, with rudder area being reduced and stabilizer area increased. Other refinements incorporated in the F–86H included a clamshell canopy and a revised cockpit layout, while the "6–3 extension" and extended wing tips were adopted as standard with effect from the 15th aircraft, although a retrospective modification programme did see slats added after the F–86H was well established in service. LABS equipment was also installed on the fifth and subsequent aircraft, but gun armament initially remained unchanged, all 113 F–86H–1s having six .50in (12.7mm) calibre machine-guns. With the appearance of the F–86H–5, a switch was made to four M39 20mm (0.8in) cannon; other weaponry

Above: In addition to the 135 F–86Fs supplied by NAA, Japan's Air Self-Defence Force received 300 F–86F–40s from Mitsubishi, of which this is the 234th example.

that could be delivered by the F–86H included tactical nuclear bombs, conventional 1,000lb (454kg) or smaller bombs, napalm canisters or up to eight five-inch (127mm) high-velocity aerial rockets, four per wing.

Two prototypes and a static test airframe were built by NAA at Los Angeles, and the first of these made its maiden flight on 30 April 1953, with company pilot Joseph Lynch in charge. Neither this nor the second machine featured armament but this was installed on subsequent F–86Hs, all of which originated at Columbus, where the first production F–86H–1 took to the air on 4 September 1953. By then, contracts had been placed for 473 aircraft, and this version began to join operational elements in autumn 1954, with TAC's 312th Fighter-Bomber Wing (FBW) at Clovis AFB, New Mexico, being the first recipient. Other F–86Hs soon found their way overseas, most notably for service with United States Air Forces in Europe (USAFE) units, where compatibility

with tactical nuclear weapons was seen as essential by the North Atlantic Treaty Organization (NATO).

TIME OF TENSION

Within a few years, however, the F–86H had gone from the front-line; but it was destined to find a welcome home with the Air National Guard (ANG). Indeed, it was while serving with the ANG that it returned to active duty on a couple of occasions. The first instance arose during the Berlin crisis of 1961–62 when a substantial number of F–86Hs deployed to Europe, and the second came in 1968 when, in the aftermath of the *Pueblo* crisis, two ANG Tactical Fighter Squadrons (104th and 138th TFS) moved to Cannon (formerly Clovis) AFB, where they performed forward air control (FAC) and combat crew training functions for a few months. Eventually, in the spring of 1970, the last of the long-serving F–86Hs gave way to the Cessna A–37B Dragonfly, thus bringing the Sabre's long and distinguished career with the USAF to a close.

Elsewhere, the Sabre was still very much alive, active as a front-line fighter with a respectable number of air arms despite the fact that it was no longer in the first flush of youth.

Above: The Royal Norwegian Air Force was one of several air arms to receive ex-USAF F–86Fs, with no less than 90 examples being supplied. Illustrated is the fourth F–86F–35 to be supplied.

Above: A major export customer for the F–86F (112 were supplied), the Republic of Korea Air Force (RoKAF) equipped its Sabres with AIM–9J Sidewinder air-to-air missiles for air defence tasks.

No attempt at relating the Sabre story would be complete without some mention of its exploits in battle, where it consistently proved superior to its opponents, despite at times being inferior in so far as its overall performance was concerned. The Korean War of 1950–53 provided the F–86 with its first exposure to combat, its main adversary in that conflict being the broadly contemporary Soviet MiG–15 "Fagot"; a small fighter possessed of similar performance characteristics and one which should have been able to meet the Sabre on more or less equal terms had the Chinese and North Korean pilots been able to claim similar flying and fighting skills to those of their US adversaries. Unfortunately for them, they were not, and what should have been a fairly evenly matched aerial battle eventually became little more than a rout, US pilots demonstrating clear-cut supremacy throughout and accounting for several hundred MiG–15 "kills" in just over two-and-a-half years of aerial combat over Korea.

In many ways, the Sabre was still very much an unknown quantity when it first went to war, the 4th FIW being hurriedly directed to move to the combat theatre from New Castle County Airport, Delaware, on 8 November 1950. That move was partly a response to the Chinese decision to commit elements of its air power to the conflict on 1 November 1950. Somewhat ironically, that occurred just a few days after General MacArthur advised

President Truman that the likelihood of Chinese intervention was low since "they have no air force" – he was soon proved wrong and UN intelligence was even more embarrassed by the appearance of the swept-wing MiG–15 on the same day, this type soon beginning to exact a heavy toll on the lumbering B–29s, although one MiG–15 was shot down by an F–80C Shooting Star piloted by Lieutenant Russell Brown in the world's first aerial engagement between opposing jet fighters.

That encounter occurred on the very day that the 4th FIW was ordered to go to war and within three days the subordinate Group had begun the long journey to Korea, its F–86As being ferried in stages to Sand Diego, California, where they were loaded aboard the escort carrier USS *Cape Esperance* and a tanker for shipment by sea. Getting under way shortly before the end of November, the 4th FIW reached Yokosuka, Japan, in mid-December, thereafter establishing a rear echelon at Johnson Air Base on

the outskirts of Tokyo and an advance echelon (Detachment "A") at Kimpo, South Korea. Operations from the latter airfield were launched on 13 December with a series of familiarization flights, and the 4th FIW opened its combat record two days later, with an uneventful orientation mission over North Korea.

SKY WARRIORS

In essence, the 4th FIW's task was that of air superiority. Fundamentally, that entailed the performance of CAP missions over north-west Korea, with the objective of preventing MiG–15s from ranging further south. At the same time, it was, whenever possible, to destroy the MiGs, but "hot pursuit" into China was expressly forbidden and many MiGs were to escape as a result of this stricture. Nonetheless, the 4th FIW wasted no time in setting about its job, Lt. Col. Bruce Hinton opening the Wing account on 17 December when he downed a MiG with a prolonged

Right: Although the F–51D Mustang could still pack a punch during the Korean War, this Second World War veteran would soon give way to the Sabre fighter-bomber.

Above: Photographed at the K–14 air base in May 1951, a quintet of 4th FIW F–86A–5s are readied for another round of action. Note the black and white ID striping.

burst of gunfire during a brief encounter above the Yalu River between four Sabres and four of the sprightly MiGs.

For the best part of a year, the 4th FIW was the only Sabre-equipped outfit in the war zone and it made good use of its exclusivity, accounting for the lion's share of the 102 MiGs claimed by the USAF during this period. For almost all of this interlude, the F–86A bore the brunt of the aerial battle, but the 4th FIW began to convert to the improved F–86E model in autumn 1951, although transition was a fairly lengthy business and some 'As lingered on in front-line service until the middle of 1952.

Partly responsible for the slow progress made was the decision to assign F–86Es as replacements for the F–80Cs

Right: Prior to joining combat, a 51st FIW F–86E pilot jettisons his external fuel tanks (note how his wingman is already "primed") and prepares to attack.

flown by another Korean-based unit. This was the 51st FIW at Suwon AB, South Korea, which received its new equipment in late November 1951 and made its combat debut with the F–86E just a few days later on 1 December. It very soon proved itself a worthy addition to the air superiority force, "bagging" 25 of the 31 confirmed victories in January 1952 and joining with the 4th FIW to account for the impressive total of 375 MiG–15s in that year.

Yet another re-equipment programme was implemented in 1952, with the definitive F–86F reaching combat elements in the summer when the 51st FIW acquired its initial examples. Three months later, it was followed by the 4th FIW, and the F–86F was also assigned to two more units during 1953. The first of these was the 18th FBW, which had previously flown the North American F–51 Mustang, logging its last sortie with this Second World War veteran fighter-bomber on 23 January 1953.

It wasted no time in beginning the conversion process, for the first three F–86Fs flew into Osan AB, South Korea, just five days later, and the 18th FBW launched its first patrol of the Yalu on 25 February in fine style

Above: Time and time again during the Korean War, Sabres flying combat air patrols would detect Communist MiG-15s and take immediate steps to intercept and engage the enemy.

when an F–86F piloted by Major James Hagerstrom claimed a MiG–15. In addition to three USAF squadrons, the 18th FBW controlled the attached No.2 Squadron, South African Air Force (SAAF), and this also received F–86Fs, joining other wing elements in battle although it seems mainly to have

Sabre at War

Above: Outflown, outfought and outgunned, the pilot inside this MiG–15 knows the game is up . . .

. . . and prepares to eject in one last-ditch attempt to escape. An explosion marks the ejection . . .

. . . and in an instant the pilot and his seat are propelled up and out of the doomed 'craft . . .

utilized the Sabre as a fighter-bomber.

Within weeks of the 18th receiving the F–86F, the 8th FBW began to follow suit, the first squadron being withdrawn from combat to enter training on 22 February, while the other two continued to use the F–80 for a little while longer, until the 80th FBS recorded the USAF's last Shooting Star combat sortie on 30 April 1952. By then, 8th FBW F–86Fs had begun operations (on 8 April) and this Wing thereafter divided its assets between MiGCAP and air-to-ground missions.

With many more Sabres available for operations, the enemy's MiG fleet took a real battering between 1 January and 27 July 1953, when hostilities terminated. Indeed, no fewer than 287 were claimed during this seven-month period, with June being a record-breaking month in almost every respect. For a start, some 77 MiGs were claimed, a figure handsomely in excess of the previous best month (September 1952 – 63 MiGs). Sortie rate also peaked (7,696), as did attrition, 14 Sabres falling foul of enemy action with nine more being lost to operational causes. In the air-to-ground arena, Sabres deposited 3,044 tons of bombs, getting on for half of the total tonnage delivered by the F–

86 in the war; but such intense activity could hardly be sustained and July was quieter, especially with regard to combat with MiGs.

Nevertheless, combat was joined on a number of occasions and the distinction of claiming the last MiG–15 to be downed in the Korean War fell to the 51st FIW's Lieutenant Sam Young on 22 July. Five days later, on the afternoon of 27 July, the 4th FIW's Captain Ralph Parr brought the air battle to an end when he shot down an Ilyushin Il–12 transport. For the Sabre, that marked the close of an illustrious chapter and its supremacy in the aerial arena is emphatically confirmed by two worthy statistics. Of 807 MiG–15s claimed in air combat by US fighters, the F–86 accounted for 792; and it also downed 18 of the 66 other enemy aircraft that were engaged by UN forces in the Korean skies.

SABRE "ACES"

Kill-loss ratios in Korea were rather one-sided and it was in that long and bloody conflict that the Sabre undoubtedly had its greatest moments of glory, this precocious newcomer to the ranks of the USAF allowing no fewer than 39 pilots to achieve the

much-vaunted status of "ace" between 20 May 1951, when Major James Jabara claimed his fifth victim, and 20 July 1953 when Major Stephen Bettinger completed the list. These 39 pilots are acknowledged to have accounted for the impressive tally of 305 enemy aircraft, almost all of which were MiG–15s, and close to 500 other MiGs were claimed by Sabre "jockeys" during more than 87,000 F–86 combat sorties logged by UN forces between December 1950 and July 1953.

In compiling that superb record, 110 F–86s are known to have fallen victim to enemy action, MiGs definitely accounting for 78 of them, while 19 were claimed by ground fire and 13 were lost to unknown causes. Other forms of attrition claimed 114 aircraft, made up of 61 to operational causes, 13 recorded as "missing" (a figure which may well include some MiG victims) and 40 to non-operational accidents, six of which actually happened at rear-echelon bases in Japan.

In any language, that must rank as a clear-cut victory for the Sabre, although it is now generally accepted that US claims erred on the generous side, with some observers being prepared to argue for an "overclaim" factor of as much as two-to-one (In this

As the Sabre's gun-camera rolls on, the MiG pilot's escape is caught on each frame of film . . .

. . . while the American fighter pumps ever more bullets into the MiG. The pilot escapes . . .

. . . but another Communist MiG fighter can be chalked up on the Sabre's "scorecard".

volume, I have chosen to use figures which appeared in a 1953 USAF analysis of the air war). In the case of the air war over Korea, however, even the most ardent protagonist of the Communist cause will find it difficult to reach any conclusion other than that the Chinese and North Korean forces took a real beating, for, even if we accept that only 400 MiGs were vanquished, the Sabre must still be viewed as markedly superior. That superiority is perhaps a classic instance of the sum being greater than the parts, for there were several factors at work which influenced the outcome.

Three of those factors were directly related to the aircraft and its systems. Performance characteristics were part of the story, the F–86F version of the Sabre possessing a narrow speed advantage at all altitudes from sea level up to service ceiling. So in the horizontal plane, the advantage clearly lay with the American fighter. When it came to the vertical plane, it was a different matter, the design philosophy behind the MiG–15 envisaging it as an interceptor rather than an air superiority fighter. In consequence, it possessed an impressive rate of climb and was able to reach 30,000ft (9,150m) in less than half the time

required by the F–86F; but that advantage was fairly easily negated, tactics evolved for Sabre pilots anxious to break off combat advocating a dive at high speed since the MiG was "redlined" at Mach.92 and was quite simply unable to continue the chase with any prospect of success.

A PILOT'S PLANE

Handling qualities also exerted considerable influence, the Sabre being rather more "user-friendly" and much less prone to spinning, while poor stall

characteristics (and a lack of stall warning) were an ever-present trap for the unwary MiG pilot. Other deficiences identified in post-war US testing of a MiG–15 revealed poor lateral and directional stability at high speed and high altitude, as well as an inferior rate of roll.

Between them, these factors worked against "carefree" handling of the MiG; unlike the Sabre which was far more amenable to vigorous control inputs, something that is confirmed by frequent allusions to "bent" aircraft, it evidently being easy to overstress an

SABRE SCORECARD

The following figures are based on the USAF Statistical Digest, Fiscal Year 1953, and cover the period from December 1950 to July 1953 inclusive.

Average number of Sabres in theatre:	**184**	
Total number of sorties flown:	**87,177**	
Number of MiGs claimed shot down:	**792**	
Other enemy aircraft claimed:	**22**	(including four on ground)
Enemy aircraft probably destroyed:	**119**	
Enemy aircraft damaged:	**818**	
Sabres lost to enemy fire:	**110**	(**78** in air-to-air combat
		19 to ground fire
		13 to causes unknown)
Non-operational losses:	**114**	

F–86 in the heat of the moment without facing the risk of it falling apart around you.

Then there was the Sabre's gunsight which utilized radar-ranging, unlike that on the MiG which was dependent on nothing more than good eyesight. Most F–86s did not, in fact, have the benefit of radar-ranging when they were built, for they were initially fitted with a Mk.18 gyro sight, but many were later updated and given the A–1CM unit which operated in conjunction with AN/APG–30 radar. An identical package was also utilized by the F–86E, but the A–1CM was distressingly prone to malfunctions and seldom bettered an "in commission" rate of around 55 per cent. With effect from the F–86f–10, an A–4 sight was standard kit and this also worked in unison with AN/APG–30 radar, but, being simpler to maintain, was much more rugged and reliable.

Two more factors also came into play in the Sabre-versus-MiG battle but it is harder to quantify the value of the contribution that they made. Training

Above: Though used primarily as an air-to-air fighter, the Sabre could also be used in a secondary role as a bomb-laden fighter-bomber, as illustrated by this South African Air Force example.

is one, the archetypal 'Sabre-driver" being the product of a better system which, while designed to instil discipline, was arguably less regimented than that of China and certainly less dogmatic. As a result, US pilots were generally more aggressive and more flexible in their approach, and they also enjoyed better morale.

Then there were tactics, and there can be no doubt that the US enjoyed an edge in this vital department, largely eschewing the escort mission which can tie up sizeable quantities of aircraft in favour of maintaining small standing combat air patrol (CAP) elements along "MiG Alley". Handily placed to deal with enemy formations heading south to disrupt other UN forces, this policy served the Sabre contingent well, even though it was often outnumbered. Nevertheless, the MiGs achieved some successes, their presence beng influential in the decision to abandon daytime Boeing B–29 Superfortress bombing raids in the autumn of 1951 when attrition rose to an unacceptable level.

BOMBS AWAY

In air-to-ground sorties, the record is less impressive, but one should not forget that the Sabre was only occassionally employed as a fighter-bomber until the 8th and 18th FBWs converted in 1953. Be that as it may, Sabres deposited 7,508 tons (7,628 tonnes) of bombs and 148 tons (150 tonnes) of napalm, and also fired 270 rockets against ground targets. These are modest figures when compared with the F–51, F–80 and F–84 which bore the brunt of ground attack duty, but Sabres did make a valuable contribution as fighter-bombers during the closing stages of the conflict. When all is said and done, though, it was as an air superiority fighter that the Sabre is best remembered, and without its presence, UN air power would have faced

Above: A graphic illustration of just how rugged the F–86 was, as Lt. Col. Robert Dixon surveys the damage inflicted on his Sabre by enemy "flak" over "MiG Alley".

almost insurmountable obstacles in furnishing support to ground forces.

Further combat between the Sabre and MiGs came in August and September 1958, when Communist China tried to impose a blockade on the islands of Quemoy and Matsu, which were occupied by Nationalist Chinese forces. By then, the heat-seeking Sidewinder AAM had been added to the Sabre's armoury and this was also put to the test, proving reasonably successful in accounting for a number of MiG–15s and MiG–17 "Frescos". Although specific details about these encounters are hard to pin down, Nationalist forces claimed the destruction of 29 MiGs at a cost of just two F–84G Thunderjets, but, once again, it seems probable that these claims were over-generous. More certain is the view that, as in Korea, pilot skill and

Left: Streaking fast and low over the target area, these Pakistan Air Force Sabres leave their "calling cards" in the highly destructive form of bombs and napalm tanks.

superior handling qualities proved to be decisive.

Pakistan's exploits with the Sabre in battle were by no means so one-sided as those of the USA or Nationalist China, but they did nevertheless add further lustre to an already impressive career and there were one or two outstanding moments in both the air-to-air and air-to-ground arenas. Foremost amongst these must surely be Squadron Leader Mohammed Mahmood Alam's epic encounter with a clutch of Indian Hunters about 30 miles (48.3km) to the east of the main Pakistani fighter base at Sargodha, on 7 September 1965.

SHOOT-TO-KILL

Then, in barely 30 seconds, he shot down four of the enemy to add to another victim claimed minutes earlier, thereby technically achieving the much-vaunted "ace" status in a single sortie, although he had in fact opened his account on the previous day when he destroyed two Hunters which intervened to prevent a strike on the Indian air base at Adampur.

Alam's adventures didn't stop there, for he subsequently accounted for two

Right: With the fruits of his aerial marksmanship recorded in the form of a most impressive "scoreboard", Sqn. Ldr. Alam comes back down to earth to face the cameras.

more Hunters in another engagement on 16 September, ending the short war as the Pakistan Air Force's top scorer with nine confirmed "kills". Eight of those were scored with the Sabre's guns, verifying that this tried and tested weapon was still a valid element of fighter aircraft armament, as indeed was the requirement to be able to shoot straight. Alam's ninth and last victim fell to a Sidewinder missile, a weapon that was treated with respect even though it was far from being as lethal as it is today.

Since Indian losses in air combat were eventually held to be about 22, Alam was personally responsible for almost half. Other Sabre pilots added to the list and the F–86 ended up victorious over about a dozen Hunters, a couple of Gnats and a quartet of de Havilland Vampires. On the debit side, Pakistan acknowledged the loss of seven Sabres in air combat but despite its age it was clear that NAA's machine was still far from being mere "cannon fodder".

In later years, the Sabre returned to battle on the side of Pakistan in 1971, while others saw a limited amount of action in service with air arms in Latin America and other "hot-spots" around the world. But it never again enjoyed such a clear-cut margin of superiority as was demonstrated in Korea.

THOSE who were intimately involved in the development of the Sabre began exploring the possibility of it performing other missions as early as 1949. At that time, it was becoming evident that the USAF interceptor programme was running into difficulties, most notably with the massive Northop F–89 Scorpion which was already several months behind schedule and which looked certain to be further delayed. Confronted with an increasingly urgent need for effective jet-powered interceptors, the authorities cast around for alternatives and soon settled on the Sabre, which had already demonstrated quite convincingly that it was by far the finest fighter available in the USA.

Alert to service needs, NAA initiated design studies on 28 March 1949, with their interceptor proposal being initially known "in house" as the NA–164. The company's initiative was very quickly rewarded when the USAF expressed interest in this derivative, and on 7 April engineering work began on the definitive production model. Referred to as the NA.165, construction of a mock-up was launched less than two months later, on 1 June 1949.

The NA.165 was significantly different, hence the decision to allocate the designation F–95 during the early stages of the development programme, although this was formally changed to F–86D with effect from 24 July 1950. Evidence of the changed role was instantly apparent if one studied the

Above: Immediately recognizeable by virtue of its large and bulbous nose radome, the F–86D "Sabre Dog" also sported a revised air intake and a retractable weapons bay.

air intake in the nose, which was now crowned by a bulbous radome housing the AN/APG–37 radar scanner which was at the heart of this version's all-weather capability. Less obvious but no less important was the decision to employ thrust augmentation as a standard feature, and all of the dedicated interceptor Sabres (F–86D/L and F–86K) were fitted with an afterburner.

Other new features which were embodied included a clamshell-type canopy hinged at the rear (both pro-

Above: A quite different aircraft from the F–86D "Sabre Dog", the awesome Northrop F–89D Scorpion was armed with 104 pod-mounted Mighty Mouse aerial rockets.

totypes had sliding canopies identical to that of the F–86A), fire control equipment courtesy of the Hughes Aircraft Company, and a vastly revised armament which consisted of 24 2.75in (7cm) *Mighty Mouse* rockets in a retractable tray located in the belly. No guns were installed, the F–86D being novel in that it was the first single-seat fighter to lack this item of armament. More significantly, it pointed the way ahead for the interceptor class of fighter, for it was too be the first to incorporate sophisticated electronic gear at the expense of a second crew member. As well as all these alterations, the F–86D had a stronger wing structure, a larger fin to compensate for the extra fuselage area and to ensure good directional stability, and additional internal fuel capacity to cope with the demands of the somewhat thirstier powerplant.

In the early stages of the develop-

ment programme, its progress was remarkably swift, with the manufacturer beginning work on a pair of prototypes in May 1949 although a formal USAF go-ahead was not actually forthcoming until 19 July. This approval was accompanied by some welcome hard cash, with the sum of $7 million being allocated to NAA in order that they might press ahead as fast as possible. Subsequently, on 7 October, the new interceptor's future was more or less assured with the award of a $79 million contract covering both of the YF–86Ds and an initial production batch of 122 F–86Ds. These were to be completed to NA.165 standard, as were a further 31 aircraft ordered in June 1950.

Of even greater significance, though, was the December 1949 decision that the F–86D would constitute the backbone of ADC's operational forces until such time as more advanced fighters like the Convair F–102 Delta Dagger (the so-called "1954 Interceptor" which did not actually enter service until the spring of 1956) became available. For NAA, selection of the Sabre interceptor paved the way

for a succession of truly massive orders, ensuing contracts for the F–86D version being placed with the company in April 1951 (for 188 aircraft), July 1951 (638), March 1952 (901) and June 1953 (624).

The momentum of this generally promising start was not destined to be maintained, and the F–86D programme suffered from quite severe slippage during the early-1950s. The fault for this lay largely outside NAA's control and was basically caused by two

factors. The first related to development problems experienced with the interim Hughes E–3 fire control system (FCS) and the even more sophisticated E–4 unit, while the second concerned General Electric's J47–GE–17 turbojet engine. In the meantime, NAA continued to churn out brand new F–86Ds by the score even though engine deliveries were running some 18 months behind schedule and electronic equipment was still in short supply. For both manufacturer and customer this was extremely irksome and for a time NAA's flight test facility at Inglewood looked more like a used aircraft lot, with well over 300 examples of the F–86D lying idle as they waited for key items of equipment to be delivered and installed.

PRODUCTION PROBLEMS

The first production-configured aircraft was formally handed over to the USAF as early as March 1951, but the difficulties already alluded to almost inevitably had a serious impact on acceptance rates and only 29 examples of the F–86D had been taken on charge by the end of June 1952. Thereafter, matters began to improve, with the latter part of Fiscal Year (FY) 1953 (July 1952–June 1953) witnessing the acceptance of some 448 aircraft. From what had been a mere trickle, the "Sabre-Dog" was now becoming available for service in a veritable flood that threatened to engulf ADC's ability to cope!

Left: A lengthened and deepened fuselage was necessary to house the F–86D's J47–GE–17 engine, but the F–86A's wings were retained.

Sabre Interceptors

With regard to operational service, the F–86D made its debut. in April 1953, almost two years behind the original target date. By way of compensation, though, the ensuing force build-up was carried through exceedingly swiftly, with the next two years witnessing the delivery of close to 2,000 more examples of the "Sabre-Dog".

After all the trials and tribulations of the previous few years, hopes were obviously running high that the new interceptor would enjoy a smooth passage as operational experience built up. Those hopes were soon to be rudely dashed, for the early period of service was by no means trouble-free, and this must have been a time of near-constant frustration for virtually everyone associated with the programme. Engine malfunctions were just one manifestation of the difficulties faced by customer and contractor alike, a rash of fires and explosions being responsible for the destruction of 13 aircraft in late-1953 and for the imposition of a fleet-wide grounding

Below: One of the initial batch of D-model Sabres, this F–86D-1 was configured for a series of research and test duties, hence the extended nose pitot. Also of note is the high-visibility colour scheme.

order while technicians from GE and NAA eradicated defects in the electronic fuel control system.

By the end of February 1954, an interim "fix" had gone some way toward resolving the engine problems, but another rash of accidents – 19 in the space of just four weeks – followed. This time the culprit was inadequate maintenance of the sophisticated weapon system which lay at the heart of the F–86D's all-weather potential. Clearly, the "beast" was in sore need of major improvement because, at that moment, it probably represented a greater threat to those who had to fly it than to an enemy.

Above: This F–86D–45 received a braking parachute on the assembly line, while Sabres already in use were retrofitted with the 'chute as part of Project "Pullout".

Project "Pullout" was the answer, this $100 million improvement initiative being designed to remedy existing faults, incorporate an extensive collection of engineering fixes and implement a number of "nice to have" modifications that had been targeted for a previously unspecified future date. What would result was a fleet of aircraft configured to a common standard, something that had thus far been sadly lacking. Responsibility for "Pullout" was entrusted to the Sacramento Air Materiel Area at McClellan AFB, California, but such was the extent of the project that much of the work was sub-contracted out to the NAA factories at Inglewood and Fresno, California.

PROJECT "PULLOUT"

Work began in March 1954 and no fewer than 1,128 F–86Ds were modified over a period of about 18 months, 648 of them at McClellan with the balance of 480 receiving attention at Fresno. The difficulty inherent in this

quite massive undertaking was compounded by the Air Force's understandable desire to complete *"Pullout"* with the minimum impact on defensive capability. The extent of this work varied but generally entailed incorporating around 300 modifications per aircraft, notable aspects of the programme including rectification of the autopilot and FCS, fitment of a radar tape system to record radar-scope data, and replacement of the original J47–GE–17 engine by the superior –17B model. In addition, aft fuselage sections were removed and despatched to Inglewood, where they were fitted with a braking parachute. Embodied as standard on production examples with effect from Block 45, the 'chute significantly reduced the length of the Sabre's landing roll.

For all its problems, the F–86D rep-

Below: Ready, aim, FIRE! In less than one-fifth of a second, all 24 of the 2.75in (70mm) Mighty Mouse aerial rockets carried within the retractable bay could be fired.

resented a very real improvement over previous interceptors, but the assistance of ground controllers was still necessary to direct aircraft to a point at which they could assume responsibility for the interception phase of a mission. The AN/APG–37 radar constituted the pilot's "eyes", scanning an arc which extended 68.5deg to the left and right of the centreline, while in elevation it could deflect 33.5deg up and 13.5deg down.

SHOOT-TO-KILL

Detection range was typically of the order of 30 miles (48.27km) and target data was displayed to the pilot by means of a small scope which was centrally positioned on the instrument panel, directly ahead of the control column. Information on this display included target range and direction, and once a pilot was satisfied that the "blip" on his screen corresponded to the target he then "locked-on" the radar. At this point, the Hughes E–4 AN/APA–84 fire-control computer

took over, automatically calculating the desired lead-collision course and providing the pilot with steering cues.

In the terminal stages of tracking, the pilot then selected how many rockets he wished to launch (options available to him were salvos of six, 12 or 24) and hit the firing button on the control column. Once again, the computer took over, performing myriad complex calculations which in essence predicted the moment at which the target would reach a particular point in space that would coincide with the arrival of the rocket armament. Once that had been established, the firing circuit was activated; the belly rocket tray was extended (this took half-a-second) and the missiles were despatched on their way, it being possible to launch all 24 Folding Fin Aerial Rockets (FFAR) in just one-fifth of a second. An "X" on the radar scope alerted the pilot to the fact that the rockets had fired, the pack then retracting automatically.

At the moment of firing, range between hunter and hunted was usually around 1,500ft (457.5m), suffi-

Sabre Interceptors

Above: The first YF–86K takes off on its maiden flight. Derived from the F–86D, it was developed to meet NATO's need for a solid and reliable all-weather interceptor.

Above: The marginal Scandinavian weather conditions led Norway to acquire 60 F–86Ks, all of which were built and supplied by NAA, as opposed to the Fiat line.

ciently close to mean that the risk of collision with either the target or debris was very real. In fine weather, with good visibility, the pilot could initiate evasive action quite easily. In murky conditions, however, it was a different matter, although the E–4 package did incorporate a collision-warning facility, a figure "8" on the display alerting the pilot to the fact that the target was less than 780ft (238m) away.

In the event of system failure, the F–86D was rendered electronically "blind". In bad weather, this naturally meant that it was virtually useless. However, in visual flight rules (VFR) conditions, it might still have been able

to inflict damage on enemy bomber aircraft, for the pilot was able to utilize an optical lead-computing sight to execute an attack.

The F–86D also served as the basis for a simplified all-weather interceptor which was developed specifically for service with a handful of NATO air arms during the 1950s and 1960s. This project had its origins in January 1953, when NAA was alerted by the Air Materiel Command (AMC) of the need for a fighter that would be essentially similar to the F–86D, using the same AN/APG–37 radar but with a less complex FCS, as well as a quartet of M–24A–1 0.8in (20mm) cannon in lieu of rocket armament, and, most significantly, a two-man crew.

THE ITALIAN JOB

In its response just a few days later, the company recommended Fiat as a suitable licensee but queried the wisdom of opting for a two-seater, arguing that this would require major redesign, a costly exercise in terms of both time and money. Instead, it proposed an airframe based on the proven F–86D (it was actually eight inches [20.32cm] longer) but with a new MG–4 FCS optimized for use with gun armament and lacking certain secret components of the E–4 package.

This recommendation found favour in high places and in May NAA was directed to proceed with the modification of two F–86Ds to serve as YF–86K prototypes. In the same month, agreement was reached with Fiat for licence manufacture of the F–86K and funding was also set aside to cover the supply of an initial batch of 50 F–86K ship-sets to be assembled in Italy. Acknowledging that it would take time to get the Italian operation up and running, the parent company was to launch F–86K production with a batch of 120 aircraft which would be assigned to the air forces of the Netherlands and Norway.

Following modification, the first YF–86K flew successfully from Los Angeles on 15 July 1954 with company test pilot Raymond Morris at the controls, and it was soon joined in the test programme by the second aircraft, both eventually being handed over to the Italians.

Last but not least, there was the F–86L, which was nothing more than a

Left: In addition to the 60 F–86Ks delivered to Norway, NAA supplied a further 59 such aircraft to the Netherlands. Many were modified to carry AIM–9 Sidewinder missiles for air defence purposes.

Right: A further refinement of the D-model produced the F–86L, 827 of which were produced. Just visible protruding from the fuselage ahead of the wing root is a small blade antenna link for the SAGE system.

converted F–86D intended to take advantage of increased automation with regard to alerting fighters to the presence of targets. At the heart of this concept was the Semi-Automatic Ground Environment (SAGE) system, which tied computers into the air defence network and which was able to transfer data electronically to airborne fighters, advising them of target heading, speed, altitude, bearing and range by means of an AN/ARR–39 data link receiver. In essence, this allowed the F–86L to be guided to a point in space at which its own E–4 FCS could assume responsibility for interception.

Modernization as part of Project *Follow-On* began in May 1956 and was accomplished by the parent company at Inglewood and Fresno, and by AMC's Sacramento Air Materiel Area at McClellan AFB. In addition to fitting new electronic components, the opportunity was also taken to incorporate the ultimate wing configuration, with 12in (30.48cm) tip extensions, "6–3" leading-edge extensions and slats combining to offer much superior handling qualities, especially when at high altitude.

Delivery of the F–86L began in October 1956, with the first ADC squadron to receive this version being the 49th FIS at Hanscom Field, Massachusetts. Just over a year later, at the end of 1957, ADC had received close to 600 F–86Ls, but plans to convert 1,240 aircraft were drastically curtailed, largely as a result of more modern interceptors like the F–102A Delta Dagger becoming available.

In ADC service, the new model remained a front-line fighter until June 1960, but quite a few ANG squadrons received "hand-me-down" aircraft from 1959 onwards and some of these units continued to fly F–86Ls until the summer of 1965, while a few aircraft found their way to Thailand.

Below: Close flying by two Royal Thai Air Force F–86Ls as seen from the cockpit of a USAF F–102 Delta Dagger. The missile rail normally carried an AIM–9 Sidewinder AAM.

ALTHOUGH the parent company was naturally responsible for the lion's share of Sabre production, licence agreements concluded with Canada and Australia culminated in manufacture of the Sabre being undertaken in both of these countries, while Italy and Japan also got in on the Sabre-building act by virtue of assembling component parts supplied by NAA. In total, these arrangements were ultimately to account for just over 28 per cent of total F–86 production, with almost 2,500 aircraft eventually rolling from factories located at Melbourne, Australia; Montreal, Canada; Turin, Italy; and Nagoya, Japan.

Overseas production was, in fact, launched by Canada, which was anxious to acquire more modern equipment in order to meet its commitments to NATO. This body came into existence in the summer of 1949 and was an influential factor in Canada's decision to buy the Sabre and to produce it locally. In consequence, an initial batch of 100 aircraft was ordered that same summer, with Canadair Ltd at Cartierville being designated as prime contractor.

In the early stages, close to 90 per cent of the Sabre was furnished to the Canadair line in the form of components and sub-assemblies, and the very first Sabre to be completed in Canada was fundamentally an F–86A–5, even though it was formally designated as the Canadair CL–13 Sabre Mk.1. Powered by a standard General Electric J47–GE–13 turbojet engine rated

Left: A stirring sight for any aviation enthusiast, as a pair of RCAF Sabre 2s head "over the top" in the company of a single RAF Hawker Hunter and a USAFE Lockheed T–33A.

at 5,200lb st (2,361kg st), this broke ground for the first time on 9 August 1950, with company test pilot Al Lilly being at the controls on this auspicious occasion.

The Sabre Mk.1 was unique, but it proved to be the forerunner of an eventual total of 1,815 aircraft, including several hundred earmarked for export under the terms of the Mutual Defense Aid Program (MDAP). Along the way, the proportion of US-supplied equipment steadily diminished, reaching a point at the end of production when some 85 per cent of each Sabre was of local origin.

Production for the Royal Canadian Air Force (RCAF) started with the Mk.2, which, in essence, was identical to the F–86E and which was also powered by the J47–GE–13 engine. Some 350 examples were completed from 1951 onwards, this quantity including 60 that were supplied to the USAF. Delivered between April and July 1952, they were known by the USAF as either the F–86E–CAN or F–86E–6 and were intended to alleviate a

Above: Virtually identical to the standard F–86E, the Canadair Sabre Mk.2 served primarily with the RCAF, although 60 units were supplied to the USAF.

Below: Delivered to the UK in bare metal, the RAF's Sabre F,4s were subsequently repainted in grey/green tactical camouflage, as exemplified by the aircraft nearest the camera.

production shortfall at a time when the Korean War was raging.

Before that, however, the Mk.2 had also joined the RCAF, with which it very quickly went abroad, No.1 Wing being despatched to RAF North Luffenham in England. Aircraft assigned to two of this organization's three squadrons (Nos. 410 and 441) were shipped across the Atlantic Ocean in 1951–52; but a new method of delivery was launched in May and June 1952 when No. 439 Squadron flew 21 aircraft over to North Luffenham in Operation "Leapfrog I". Thereafter, aerial delivery became standard operating procedure, subsequent "Leapfrog" operations witnessing the transfer of No.2 Wing (Nos. 416, 421 and 430 Squadrons) over to Grostenouin, France, in autumn 1952; No.3 Wing (Nos. 413, 427 and 434 Squadrons) to Zweibrucken, West Germany, in 1953; and No.4 Wing (Nos. 414, 422 and 444 Squadrons) to Sollingen, West Germany, also in 1953.

Hard on the heels of the Mk.2 came the Mk.4, no fewer than 438 examples being churned out at Dorval in 1952–1953, and differing only slightly in detail. All were produced to satisfy MDAP obligations, the Canadair Sabre having been selected to enter service with the RAF which was due to receive 430 in total, 370 of these being funded by Canada and 60 by the USA. As it turned out, the retention of test specimens and some pre-delivery attrition claimed a total of 10 airframes. Loss of these aircraft meant that production was extended slightly, but 428 examples did eventually reach the RAF, where they were known as Sabre F.4s.

Three other Canadair Sabres also wore RAF insignia, a trio of Mk.2/F.2s being amongst the initial batch to be delivered, although the first of these was eventually returned to Canada. When the deliveries got underway in December 1952, RCAF experience with "Leapfrog" had confirmed that aerial ferrying was feasible and this method was used for the entire block, all of which were successfully flown across the Atlantic Ocean in the space of just over one year as part of Operation "Becher's Brook".

The majority of RAF Sabres were assigned to elements of NATO's 2nd Tactical Air Force (2 TAF) in West Germany, units that operated the type comprising Nos. 3, 4, 20, 26, 67, 71, 93, 112, 130 and 234 Squadrons. In addition, two Fighter Command squadrons (Nos. 66 and 92) also had Sabres for a spell, operating these from RAF Linton-on-Ouse in Yorkshire, and it is interesting to note that the funding source for these MDAP machines had a definite bearing as to where they were assigned. Thus, Canadian-financed examples found their way to Germany, while the 60 US-funded aircraft were specifically allotted to Fighter Command.

Even though production of the Mk.2 and Mk.4 kept Canadair busy, work on a rather different model of the Sabre made steady progress and this, like the Sabre Mk.1, was to prove a "one-off". Known as the Sabre Mk.3,

Above: While the vast majority of the 431 Canadair Sabre F.4s for the RAF went to 2 TAF in West Germany, 60 examples were assigned to Nos. 66 **and 92 Squadrons, Fighter Command. Adding a dash of colour to this particular aircraft are the red and yellow checks of the latter unit.**

Above: The arrival of the Hawker Hunter rendered the Sabre F.4 all but obsolete in RAF service. The vast majority were subsequently **completely overhauled and passed on secondhand to Italy (180 examples, one of which is shown here) and to Yugoslavia (112 examples).**

Above: Incorporating the "6–3" extended wing, as well as the more powerful Orenda 10 engine, the Canadair Sabre 5 proved to be a highly potent performer.

the aircraft concerned utilized an Avro Orenda 3 turbojet engine. Rated at 6,000lb st (2,724kg st), this was significantly more powerful than the original J47, and the Mk.3 was later to be used by Jacqueline Cochran when she established two women's world speed records at Edwards AFB in 1953.

ENGINE EXCHANGE

Development of the Mk.3 was, however, not merely intended to provide a "record-breaker", for it had long been Canadair's intention to use the Canadian-built Orenda engine in the Sabre, and NAA had modified a standard F–86A–5 to take the new engine as early as October 1950. Test results soon revealed that notable performance benefits accrued, but Canadair's hopes of fitting the Orenda to the Mk.4 were shelved and it fell to the Sabre Mk.5 to emerge as the first production version to utilize this powerplant as standard.

Known by the manufacturer as the CL–13A, the latest Sabre model was actually fitted with the Orenda 10 engine which was rated at 6,500lb st (2,951kg st). It also differed in other ways, not least of which was the adoption of the "6–3" extended leading-edge and wing fences that were first introduced during production of the F–86F by NAA in the USA. Assembly of the first Sabre 5 was completed on 21 July 1953, and this aircraft made its maiden flight just nine days later, very quickly demonstrating superior performance, epitomized by the fact that it could climb to 40,000ft (12,200m) in half the time taken by the Sabre 2. The switch to the so-called "hard wing" did, however, have a detrimental effect on stability at low speeds, with the stalling speed increasing by about 20mph (32km/h), and it was to restore low-speed qualities that led to slats being reintroduced on the ultimate Canadair CL–13B Sabre Mk.6.

In the meantime, production of the Sabre 5 continued, some 370 examples eventually being completed, including 75 that were supplied to West Germany's rejuvenated Luftwaffe. Manufacture then turned to the Mk.6 derivative, which was easily the most powerful of all the Canadian Sabres by virtue of being fitted with an Orenda 14 turbojet engine rated at 7,275lb st (3,303kg st). With 655 aircraft completed, it was also easily the most numerous variant.

SALES SUCCESS

Initial specimens retained the "hard wing" of the Mk.5, but this was soon supplanted by extended, slatted wings and production commenced with 292

Below: Forever associated with the Sabre, the RCAF's *Golden Hawks* display team operated Sabre 6s aptly painted in a striking overall gold colour scheme.

Sabres Overseas

Above: Of the 655 Sabre 6s built by Canadair, six were supplied to the Colombian Air Force in 1956, making them the first Sabres to be acquired by a South American country. Along with five F–86Fs from NAA, the Sabre served the Colombian Air Force until retirement in 1979.

Above: In purely numerical terms, the reborn German Luftwaffe was the second-largest customer for the Sabre (after the RCAF), with no less than 225 Mk.6s acquired. The mid-fuselage "R" crest identifies this as a Sabre assigned to Jagdgeschwader (Fighter Group) 71 *"Richthofen"*.

Above: An altogether different set of camouflage colours highlights the contrast in climates of Northern Europe and Southern Africa, this being one of 34 Sabre 6s to serve with the South African Air Force (SAAF). Acquired to replace F–86Es, they served until the early-1970s.

aircraft for the RCAF, with the first machine being completed on 2 November 1954. Some 40 export examples followed, spearheaded by half-a-dozen for Colombia, all of which were handed over in June 1956, with the remainder going to South Africa. RCAF contracts were then completed with a further batch of 98 aircraft before production terminated with no fewer than 225 for the Luftwaffe. Other customers had also been anxious to obtain the Sabre 6, Argentina being forced to cancel its order for 36 when it discovered that it would be unable to pay for them. Israeli plans anticipated the purchase of 24 aircraft, and some pilots were under training in Canada in 1956 when hostilities erupted between Israel and neighbouring Arab states. Inevitably, an arms embargo ensued and Israel never did operate the Sabre, turning to France as a rich source of military hardware and support for the next decade or so.

ONE-OFF WONDERS

For Canadair, that was just about it as far as developing the Sabre was concerned, although brief mention should be made of a number of interesting projects which failed to reach fruition, even though some of them progressed as far as the flight test stage. Most were aimed at enhancing performance still further and they included the CL–13C with an afterburner to boost Orenda 14 power; the CL–13D with an Armstrong–Siddeley Snarler rocket motor; the CL–13E with an area-ruled fuselage; the CL–13G two-seat trainer; the CL–13H with all-weather radar; and the CL–13J with a Bristol-designed afterburner. Of these, only the CL–13C and CL–13E were evaluated in flight, and the fact that neither was proceeded with seems to confirm that the benefits they offered were considered marginal at the very best.

CANADAIR PRODUCTION

Sabre Mk. 1	19101	**1**	(from F–86A parts)
Sabre Mk. 2	19102–199	**98**	
	19201–452	**252**	(including 60 F–86E–6–CAN to USAF as 52–2833/892 and three to RAF)
Sabre Mk. 3	19200	**1**	(Orenda-powered prototype)
Sabre MK. 4	19453–890	**438**	(All for RAF including US-funded machines with US identities 52–10177/236)
Sabre Mk. 5	23001–370	**370**	(including 75 for Luftwaffe)
Sabre Mk. 6	23371–760	**390**	
	2021–2026	**6**	(Colombian AF)
	350–383	**34**	(South African AF)
	1591–1815	**225**	(Luftwaffe)
	Total quantity 1,815		

Canadian production of the Sabre was quite clearly a massive undertaking, as well as a hugely successful one. In contrast, Australia's contribution to the Sabre saga was relatively small, just 112 examples being completed and all of these earmarked for service with the Royal Australian Air Force (RAAF), although some were later passed on to other air arms operating in the southern hemisphere.

FUTURE PLANS

While it may not have scored heavily in terms of quantity, there can be little doubt that Commonwealth Aircraft Corporation (CAC) versions underscored the Sabre's adaptability, utilizing a new engine and different armament which necessitated quite significant modifications to the basic structure. Australia's decision to buy the Sabre was confirmed on 22 February 1951, and was largely prompted by involvement in the Korean War where No.77 Squadron Gloster Meteors were having a somewhat lean time.

Right: Caught on the flightline at Butterworth, Malaysia, this RAAF Sabre Mk. 32 receives the attentions of groundcrew prior to conducting an anti-terrorist sortie.

While it might have been cheaper in the short-term to buy "off the shelf", the RAF was anxious to obtain a durable and long-serving machine, and this had quite a marked influence on the outcome, Australian Sabres differing notably from their US counterparts in that they were all powered by a Rolls-Royce Avon RA.7 turbojet rated at 7,500lb st (3,405kg st). While it bestowed a number of worthwhile performance benefits, installation of this engine also dictated some redesign. By way of illustration, the mass airflow requirements could only be satisfied by inserting a 3½in (9cm) splice in the air intake so as to offer increased area. In addition, the different dimensions and weight of the Avon required that it be mounted further aft in order to satisfy centre of gravity criteria, and this in turn affected the fuselage breakpoint location.

GUNS, GUNS, GUNS

Other changes concerned armament, initial plans calling for a quartet of 20mm (0.8in) cannon. In August 1952, however, it was decided to use a pair of Aden 30mm (1.1in) guns

Sabres Overseas

Above: Selected in preference to Britain's Firestreak air-to-air missile, the American AIM–9 Sidewinder notably enhanced the CAC Sabre's fighting prowess.

Fishermen's Bend to Avalon, which was the centre for all experimental and production testing. Almost one year elapsed before a second example got airborne, making its maiden flight on 13 July 1954, and this was the first of the type to be formally handed over to the RAAF, by coincidence exactly one year after the prototype ventured skyward on its initial flight. This, and all the other 110 RAAF Sabres, were designated as CA–27s

Production of the initial batch of Sabre Mk.30s totalled 21, and aircraft from this block began to join the service trials unit at Williamtown, New South Wales, shortly before the end of

1954. Development and service testing kept these aircraft fully occupied for the next year or so and it was not until 1 March 1956 that the Sabre was elevated to operational status when No.3 Squadron, RAAF, took delivery of its first production examples.

UPGRADING

A subsequent retrofit project involving the surviving Mk.30s brought them up to Mk.31 standard and entailed fitment of the extended "hard wing"; but further production also accounted for a further 21 Mk.31s, two of which were given additional

Above: Rendered surplus to the operational requirements of the RAAF by Dassault Mirage IIIs, 16 CAC-built Sabre 32s found a new lease of life courtesy of the Royal Malaysian Air Force. Ten were delivered in October 1961, and six more in 1971.

instead, which, in concert with a revamped cockpit layout, increased fuel capacity. At the same time, a new engine start system forced CAC to redesign roughly 60 per cent of the Sabre structure. That the effort was worthwhile is perhaps best confirmed by the fact that the Sabre survived as a front-line RAAF fighter until as recently as the early-1970s, and that quite a few continued to give good service in Indonesia and Malaysia for several years after that.

The first Australian Sabre was put together largely from US-supplied components and given the designation CA–26. Powered by an imported Avon engine, it took to the sky for the first time on 3 August 1953, having been moved by road from the factory at

Above: During their career with the Royal Malaysian Air Force, extant Sabres had their natural metal finish replaced by this more sober camouflage. Trusted and faithful warriors to the end, they had given way to Northrop F–5E Tiger IIs by 1980.

fuel capacity by virtue of a "wet" leading-edge which housed 70 US gal (265 litres) of fuel. Thereafter, CAC turned its attentions to the definitive Mk.32, which was fitted with the Australian-built Avon 26 and which also featured "dual-store" wings and "wet" leading-edges containing 60 US gal (227 litres) of fuel. Some 69 Mk.32s were completed, most of them later being "wired" to take the Sidewinder infra-red homing air-to-air missile (AAM). This weapon was introduced on Australian Sabres in 1960, being adopted in preference to the British Firestreak AAM.

CAC PRODUCTION		
CA–26	A94–101	1*
CA–27 Mk. 30	A94–901/921	21
CA–27 Mk. 31	A94–922/942	21
CA–27 Mk. 32	A94–943/990	48
	A94–351/371	21
Total quanitity 112		

*(mainly from NAA components)

ORIENTAL ORDERS

Other agreements related to the Sabre were concluded with Italy and Japan, but these concerned assembly of components provided by NAA rather than outright manufacture. Nevertheless, they accounted for an additional 521 aircraft, and no account of Sabre history would be complete without some mention of them. Looking at Japan first, the Japanese Air Self-Defence Force (JASDF) received an initial batch of 180 F–86Fs direct

Right: Originally supplied to the JASDF, the farthest of these two F–86Fs was one of 45 returned to the USA as local production grew. It was then passed to South Korea.

from the USA between December 1955 and December 1956, although a shortage of qualified pilots and the increasing availability of locally-assembled aircraft eventually resulted in 45 of them being handed back to the USA in February 1959.

Even as the last of the US-built machines was being handed over, so too were the first aircraft assembled by Mitsubishi at its Nagoya factory, from where the first local Sabre undertook its maiden flight on 9 August 1956. Barely five weeks later, on 20 September, this aircraft was delivered to the JASDF, with three more examples following from Mitsubishi by the end of

Above: Delivered to Japan as an F–86F–30, this Sabre became one of 18 camera-equipped RF–86Fs for the JASDF. One K–17 and two K–22 cameras were installed.

the year. All were covered by a contract for 70 aircraft that was concluded between the Japanese company and NAA on 28 June 1956, and later contracts upped the ante quite considerably. The first of these was signed on 28 September 1956 and covered 110 sets of Sabre parts, with Japanese assembly being completed by a third batch of 120 aircraft contracted for on 24 April 1958.

Sabres Overseas

Between them, these orders kept Mitsubishi occupied until 25 February 1961, when the 300th and last Sabre was completed, formal delivery of this and two other machines bringing the project to a close just two days later, roughly a year behind schedule due to typhoon damage sustained at the Nagoya factory in September 1959. By then, the JASDF was one of the world's largest Sabre operators, for it also received 122 F–86D all-weather interceptors from the USAF between 1958–61, retaining some of these in its front-line inventory until late-1968.

FINAL FLIGHTS

Of the day fighters, 18 of the original US-supplied machines were modified to perform photo-reconnaissance tasks as RF-86Fs, and a few of these remained active until October 1979. The pure fighter version lingered on as an operational type until 1980 and in second-line tasks until March 1982, when aircraft 62–7497 made its final flight. Following withdrawal, most JASDF Sabres were simply scrapped, but quite a few did find their way back to the USA for use as QF–86F drones by the US Navy from the Naval Weapons Center at China Lake, California, and the Pacific Missile Test Center at NAS Pont Mugu, also in California.

Above: The red on natural metal scheme betrays the JASDF life of this Sabre, although it now serves as a QF–86F pilotless target drone at Naval Weapons Center China Lake, Ca.

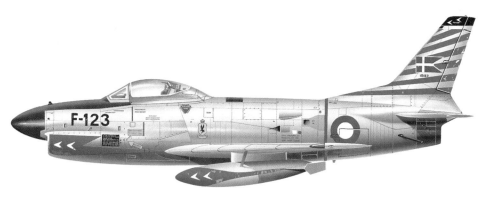

Above: Rendered obsolete by the arrival in service of Convair's F–102A Delta Dagger, a number of F–86Ds found new life with the Royal Danish Air Force. In all, 56 "Sabre Dogs", including this F–86D–35 serving with Eskadrille 726, were acquired.

Above: While Denmark acquired its F–86Ds from the USA, the Turin assembly line in Italy was the source for 88 F–86Ks supplied to the West German Luftwaffe. Note the high-visibility fuel tanks and the Jagdgeschwader (Fighter Group) 74 fin crest.

Italy's contribution to Sabre production was limited to 221 aircraft, all of which were F–86K all-weather interceptors, a variant that is more fully described in Chapter Four. Funded by MDAP, agreement for assembly of these machines by Fiat was reached on 16 May 1953, and the first example to be completed by this company made a successful maiden flight just over two years later, on 23 May 1955. By that time, however, testing of a pair of YF–86K prototypes (both modified F–86Ds) had been under way in the USA for almost a year, and manufacture of

Above: Of the 221 F–86K kits supplied to Fiat for assembly, 63 went on to serve with the Aeronautica Militare Italiana (Italian Air Force), including these 51 Stormo examples.

120 aircraft was also well advanced, delivery of these to Norway and the Netherlands beginning in June 1955.

With regard to the Turin-assembled F–86Ks, deliveries started in 1956, with the Italian Air Force acquiring 63 as well as both of the YF–86K prototypes. Half-a-dozen examples found their way to the Netherlands, and Norway obtained four, but the bulk of the remaining production went to France, which received 60 in 1957, and West Germany, which took delivery of 88 in 1958, the final 45 being completed with extensions to their leading-edges and wingtips.

As it transpired, not all German aircraft saw operational service, Jagdbombergeschwader 74 (JG 74) being the only unit to use the F–86K. Of the non-operational F–86Ks, about three dozen were held in storage at Oberpfaffenhofen, near Munich, for several years, these eventually being disposed of to Venezuela, which obtained just over 50 from West Germany in 1967–68. Some survivors remained in use with the South American nation until about 1981, while a few were resold to Honduras in 1969.

Above: Sadly, a blow torch in a scrap yard all too often marked the final chapter in a Sabre's story. Yet no-one can deny it was a true legend of the skies.

SABRE OPERATORS BY MODEL

Country	A	D/L	E	F	H	K	CL–13	CA–27
Argentina				●				
Australia								●
Belgium				●				
Bolivia				●				
Burma				●				
Canada							●	
Colombia							●	
Denmark		●						
Ethiopia				●				
France						●		
Greece		●						
Holland						●		
Honduras			●	●		●		
Indonesia								●
Iran				●			●	
Iraq				●				
Italy						●	●	
Japan		●		●				
Malaysia								●
Norway				●		●		
Pakistan				●			●	
Peru				●				
Philippines		●		●				
Portugal				●				
Saudi Arabia				●				
South Africa				●			●	
South Korea		●		●				
Spain				●				
Taiwan		●		●				
Thailand		●		●				
Tunisia				●				
Turkey		●					●	
United Kingdom							●	
US Air Force	●	●	●	●	●		●	
US Army							●	
US Navy				●	●			
Venezuela				●		●		
West Germany						●	●	
Yugoslavia		●					●	

Notes: Iraq and Belgium only received a few F–86Fs and soon disposed of them.
Greek, Italian, Turkish and Yugoslavian CL–13s were known as F–86E(M) after refurbishment.
CL–13s in USAF use were designated F–86E–6–CAN.
US Army CL–13s are configured as drone targets.

INDEX